salmonpoetry

Publishing Irish & International
Poetry Since 1981

Among the Gliesians
PHILIP FRIED

This collection is published in 2020 by
Salmon Poetry, Cliffs of Moher, County Clare, Ireland
www.salmonpoetry.com   email: info@salmonpoetry.com

Copyright © Philip Fried, 2020

ISBN 978-1-912561-83-4

Cover & Title Page Photography: *Lynn Saville*
Cover Design & Typesetting: *Siobhán Hutson*
Printed in Ireland by Sprint Print

To Lynn, with all my love

Contents

I.

Seven Rounds

Man's Best Friend

Untamed, they aimlessly wandered the ancient forests
that surrounded human settlements, until
lured by the fragrance of cooking meat and the cunning
of the hand that ignited the fire, they poked their muzzles

into human affairs and began to co-
evolve with our motor cortex and fingers, quickly
warming to the role of loyal sidekick
of the master whose fist can grip opportunity,

and learning that while targets can be chosen
for nothing more than spite, or a laugh, or belief,
the aim in every case must still be true,
and this is how the domesticated breeds

were engendered, so that when the right hand
of the sole survivor, held aloft, is the last
of him to enter a manhole, in it will nuzzle
a Glock or Beretta, to the end steadfast.

What Goes Around ...

Align the front and back gun-sights
To change things as they seem.
Ease ease ease the trigger.
Life is but a dream.

A gun range, a sunny sky
"Live" target zombies with limbs awry
In an afternoon of July.

Children three who are begging for more,
Eager to improve their score,
Pleased to learn about gun lore.

Long has paled that sunny sky:
Echoes fade and memories die.
Autumn frosts have slain July.

Still they haunt me, metal spinner;
Abstract targets smaller/bigger;
Nasty-man profile and fearsome critter.

Children learning to clean the gun barrel
Embrace the direction that's natural,
Lubricate as the bullet would travel.

In the Wonderland Range they vie
Dreaming of scoring rings, bullseye,
Dreaming as the summers die.

Elfin Alice soon, with a 20-
(Learner's) gauge shotgun, bagged her quarry.
Late ears and whiskers. End of story.

"Print the Legend"

This is the West, sir. When the legend becomes fact ...

—*The Man Who Shot Liberty Valance*

The sheer unendingness of slaughter, its far
horizon, has emptied the land of Others and buffalo,
so with nothing more to foster, the murderous
and murdered dust will journey in every direction
via the light beam of a movie projector

to simulate cowtowns in grade B films, where cards
are fate, aces and eights, the dead man's etc.,
and every stained round table, an omphalos
as hands deal hands to hands and player pianos
handless assault the music of the spheres,

celebrity being our brand of Calvinism,
the elect chosen by the blessèd bestowal
of renown, to have a name, for good or ill,
to be a big noise, or cheese, or macher, but to be
known! Gunslinger, Gambler, Preacher, Madam,

and the Just Plain Folks, the Pistols, lighting out
for the territories, Remi, Colt, and even
that lady's man and gambler, Deringer,
adepts of a frontier's peppery repartee,
salt of the earth, who will sow the earth with salt.

How Often Must We Repeat ...

Mass shootings will naturally trigger public alarm,
Their innocent victims are enshrined in our prayers,
But it's people not guns that finally cause the harm.

To deal with irrational evil, be practical:
If you carry a gun, you'll never be caught unawares,
Though shootings will naturally trigger public alarm.

The truth is on high, that's why we're devotional.
Direct your gaze skyward, be the one who dares ...
Intone: God knows, it's people that cause the harm.

Ban guns and a knife attack would be probable.
Without our concealed weapons, we're helpless hares.
Mass killings will naturally trigger public alarm.

The knee-jerk response of the left is gun control.
The innocent Glock and AK are liberals' bugbears,
But it's people not guns that finally cause the harm.

New laws should focus on the mentally ill,
Those Others who are the stuff of our worst nightmares.
Mass shootings will naturally trigger public alarm,
But it's nutty people, not guns, that cause the harm.

Jumping the Gun

He took it too much to heart when they called him a "pistol"
but never imagined that machined aluminum
would begin replacing the muscle in a ventricle.
(He figured arrhythmia, that's what I'm suffering from.)

Meantime his lifeblood flowed into his handgun,
which now was muscle and every shot heartfelt.
At last he truly carried his heart, if not on
his sleeve, then close on his right side though well

concealed. *No more a shot in the dark,* his credo:
He'd train! And the brainstorm — it caused his stomach to flutter —
that came to him in a flash: he needed more ammo!
If he could keep that idea in his mind's chamber,

spin past dizziness into the eye of the storm,
and aim for the inner light ... *Get a grip,* they told him.

Creative Policing

I lost my identity, she confessed
to the desk sergeant,
it was in my wallet, stolen
last Saturday night in Jersey City,
but I'm not worried about the wallet, no,
it's that I have to fly home
to Florida early tomorrow
and I have no identity

listen,
can't we get creative
you have my fingerprints on file,
can't you check mine against them and write
a letter to the airline saying
I am who I am,
she is who she is, you know,
so I can fly home?

to which the sergeant replied
let me get this straight, let
me break this down:
last Saturday? in Jersey City?
and now? in New York? you want *us* ...?
umm hmmm!
and the veteran walls, faded green
in color but strong in support,
agreed

next in line was a hesitant
partly stooped middle-aged man
concerned about his sharp knives
he wanted to dispose of them as soon
as possible but
you'd arrest me if you caught
me walking out on the street, a danger

to others and maybe
myself you might assume, with my very sharp knives
so I thought, let me come here,
to them, they'll tell me, to you ...

to which the sergeant, half listening while
gazing at his screen saver, replied
with a finely calibrated disdain
sir
we don't take knives, we take guns
and was seconded by his oblong blotter

Voice

"Voice is a pretty amazing thing," said the lead
researcher for an experiment to implant

connective tissue and lining cells from healthy
vocal cords into the muzzle of a jammed

Kalashnikov, reviving the keen patter
of one whose speech had unexpectedly faltered.

"We don't give voice much thought until it goes wrong,"
he added. "It's an exquisite system and hard

to replicate." When the transplanted folds of tissue
in the AK were triggered, they spoke with the same penetration

as a normal forceful voice and therefore could pierce
irrelevant objections of walls or of common

vehicles' metal bodies equally well.
And cogent arguments remained intact

even after making contact with bone.
Moreover, scientists believe the immune

systems of any faltering weaponry
will soon accept vocal cords taken from dead human donors.

Best of all, high-speed digital imaging
revealed the Kalashnikov had endured the scaffolds

of tough elastic tissue without failing
to cycle, and was uttering bursts of words

on the tactics and techniques of debate; for example,
I commence my case with an attention-grabber.

Or, *To better rebut my opponents' contention,
I remember to cluster sub-points closely together.*

II.

Among the Gliesians

Ethnographic reports on the Gliesians [GLEE zhunz],
inhabitants of the planet Gliese [GLEE zuh],
which orbits a red dwarf star 20 light-years from Earth.

A Planetary Pastime

My informant brought me to a stadium-crater
where fans gather to follow Rubble Wrestling.

Cattycornered, facing off against
each other, two rocks begin to utter mouthless
curses, vehement as the planet's molten
primordial core, while remaining — somehow — inert
(the crowd is transfixed by the stunning bitterness
of minerals). Here is a typical clip
from the classic bout between F. Spar and Q. Artz,
contenders from the continental crust —
each an avatar for his mineral nation,
the former splendid in his beige "spandex,"
the latter flipping a crystal "middle finger":

Igneous bastard, I'll send you crying back
to your magma!
           Not before I pound you silly,
you high-silica cry-baby!
           You flux,
you alkali, you sanitaryware
filler!
           I'll decimate your diasterism! ...

The goal of the sport is the utter obliteration
of the other and yet (although the mesmerized fans
watch for hours, debate the merits and import
of every taunt, depart from the arena
at night, but return the next day eager as ever)
no one has seen the rocks collide and wrestle,
and anyone will confide to you, sotto voce,
that such an event would shake the fabric of space-
time itself, and is unimaginable.

Later, I shall have more to say about
passivity ratios in the balance between
risk and spectacle among the Gliesians.

A Favorite Indoor Sport

Headline Climbing, a favorite indoor sport
and schooling for leaders, involves a handful of simple
drills to perfect the nuances of footwork
when ascending a mock-up of routes and boulder problems
studded with foothold jibs, small divots, flows
of handholds in wave designs, and natural features
on the wall — all curiously tagged with headlines.

Encountering a "pocket" with screamer, No
Evidence to Support the Leader's Claims,
the climber is expressly instructed to cling
to the wall by sticking a pointed toe in the opening,
then pressing down forcibly with the forefoot and raising
the heel slightly to engage the calf.

To establish a foothold on an expanse of "flatwall"
blazoned, Resuming the Deportation of All
Who Are Other, the climber should smear his foot as if
on a slab, dropping the heel to maximize contact
and bending toes upward bringing the forefoot to bear.

When ascending to the "small edge" stigmatized, Sharing
Inflammatory Anti-Alien Videos,
the climber will focus on the narrowest section
of this scanty hold, ankle perpendicular.

For a "sloper" bannered, Denying Obstruction Specter,
the climber drops the heel and pushes on toes
to maximize contact and stay up high on the hold.

Finally, a well-schooled speck in the ceiling's heaven,
the climber will preen for a time in this easeful empyrean,

then descend, keen for an arduous real-world climb ...

A Graveyard of Past Futures

The Gliesian language, known as "Glie," allows
for a linking of tenses dizzying to an earthling
but justified by the Gliesian concept of GLEW,
an acronym based on words that refer to a fluid
fourth dimension and are now forgotten.

All stories commence with this phenomenological
mantra: "As a composite of many
present tenses, now past ..." [For the full text
of this formula, see the appendix, which also describes
the surprising appeal this mouthful has for children.]

A popular national theme park is named, A Graveyard
of Past Futures. Among its many features
are the severed sculpted hand with Liberty's torch
and a tapeloop of age-old clips from leaders' speeches
promising a better tomorrow, tomorrow ...

In photos on gravestones, re-enactors revive,
in costume, the daily doings of communes
and utopian farms, their sepia hopes well-framed,
and navigating the clutter-maze of packaging
in which the gadgets of Progress were purveyed

is a fun adventure in found and lost. While tucked
away in the crannies and nooks of mausoleums,
sleek models of tomorrow's metropolis
prove futurism is truly a form of nostalgia
in plaster, a pseudo-alabaster whisper.

A Singular Sect

Scattered in outlying settlements across
this planet-nation are the Emotikites,
a sect that strives for a wordless paradise
by communicating solely via emojis,
emoticons, and texting abbreviations.

In prayer, they pace a Circle of Negation
widdershins, while chanting acronyms
like OON and ROV (Obliteration of Nouns
Revoking of Verbs) that have come unmoored from their words.

The E's exhibit a bipolar alternation
between celibacy and promiscuity.
In the former condition, they riffle imaginary
pages of their "Good Air-Book" to cite
parables extolling the holy and pure
and in the latter phase, the initial approach
to a possible partner is made via emophone,
a high-tech device that facilitates the exchange
of e-crotch photos and emoticon "poems."
(A rare apostate Emotikite, an elder,
has promised to reveal more about wordless
sexting, its misty origins. I'll probe him.)

Like Essenes of our own biblical times,
but with a Gliesian twist, E's fervently wish
to merge with He/She who can be iconized
but not named. And their faith leads them to shun
the weaker ones among them who caught between worlds
squat by the roadside begging for one or two words.

An Ethnographic Fieldnote

Place and Time: Caldera Anteroom
of the Dormant Volcano Cafe; early AM.
Informant: retired Charadist, an elder. *Below,*
elaborate on the cultural role of this caste
of semi-professional mimes and demi-prophets.
He's thin and bald, with a salt-and-pepper beard
whose tips keep dipping into his stein of New
Hyperonian Brew, its bubbles appearing to wink
as he whispers, "At birth, we're given the gist of a Message
that must be conveyed wordlessly, through gesture."

He leans forward, further bathing his beard,
confides that while his father had warned him, Never
— *note psychic artifacts of Oedipal*
effects — get ahead of yourself, "the problem
is, I never got far enough ahead!"
Now that he's in "the limbo of dormancy"
he can disclose his two-word Message — Falling
Upward — "a pith without a periphery."
Explore Charadists' use of paradox
as a bridge across a cultural abyss.

Wistfully reminiscing, claims he busked
on the gritty pavement stages of city corners,
performing a headlong stumble with flailing arms
that lofted him into flight. *Is this possible?*
Validate with videotapes. And later,
earned his living in media, simultaneously
interpreting and rebutting neon-wigged leaders
through the sheer physicality of "counter-contortions."
Like the signers who gesture beside our politicians?
His audience: "Any stray soul who can read a body."

As speakers blast the latest pop hit, *Eruptions,*
he gazes down at his brew's "*unheimlich* foam,"
in which he sees "a shock of whitened hair,
an age-old pattern, frothy with entropy" —
analyze strand of primitive animism —
and falls into a stupor.
       [Here, note breaks off ...]

An Issue for Further Research

Is it a noble attribute or an addiction,
this passion of Gliesian men for folded flags?
Working in teams that strive for the strictest creases
ensuring that stars on a blue field can be seen
on a tight-folded cloth to be clutched between heart and hand.
As someone's deployed to an absence more profound
for every rigorous fold that hands enforce,
uncannily this addiction and this loss
are the source not only of mourning but also of pride
and the bugle's unfolding of Taps over cratered hillside.

An Age of Diplomacy

On the planet Gliese, the cratered landscape reveals
the ravages of frequent wars and yet
Gliesians take special pride in the high art
of diplomacy, refined to a Kabuki-like
perfection. On screens, they watch two other screens
facing each other, each with one right hand
grasping air in the pantomime of a firm
handshake of fellowship across the gap
of air. Then, the mirroring hands perform
intimate alpha gestures (in the absence
of actual bodies); for instance, the guiding-palm-
of-the-host or encouraging-knuckle-nudge-to-rib
of Gliesian bromance. An icon of this Age
of Diplomacy is the hologram of a grin
whose width is pieced together from many small smiles
eeked out from diplomats of the aggrieved parties
and which hovers like a mobile in the Great
Hall of the Spectacle of Winning the Peace.
Most striking, and reserved for a time of imminent
crisis that diplomats, abject and proud,
dread and crave at once is the apparition
of the bristling white mustache, devoid of a mouth,
that conjures visions of the aftermath
of nuclear war, victims vaporized
to shadow. Informants were vehement this horrific
threat was unlikely to be carried out
now the apparition is so well produced
and their elected elders schooled to resist
the admitted allurements of omnipotence.

III.

Operating on the Body Politic

Fabricating Uncertainty

Doubt is our product.

— Hill and Knowlton, the pr firm representing
the tobacco industry, 1953-1968

The pinnacle of the art and the most
time-consuming part is the stitching
of hyper-fine thread as molten pig
iron is poured from a blast furnace
into openwork fabric, the holes
admitting argon or nitrogen
bubbled into the ladle to make
scores of intricate minuscule stitches
that with fluxes in the vessel
form an emulsion, if executed
deftly by needle or, nearly as good,
by bobbin and pillow, and mixed correctly
left over right and right over left,
link the Old French *las*, which is noose,
to Latin *lacere*, ensnare or entice,
when highly pure oxygen's introduced
at supersonic speed through the lance,
producing doubt in industrial bulk
while reflecting an artisan's flair for gossamer.

Redaction

It blindfolds the reader who, reborn
as a child at a birthday party, plays
pin the tail on someone or someplace
ridiculous, in the confusion.

    •

It blindfolds the text so it brays
vaguely
and strays from page to page
without giving testimony.

    •

It accoutres the guards in unrippable
black fabric as well as a face
mask with a visor, to shield detainees
from encounters that are too personal.

    •

Truth, they say, is a broken-down nag, one step
ahead of the glue factory.
These blinkers will spare it from the fret-
fulness of glimpsing a grim periphery.

    •

Concealed by a neo-classical facade,
this office has hosted covert
chirping re wetwork code-named Cricket
and Katydid — stridulations strictly classified.

    •

Overlook the creator's rumored infractions,
secreted in the endlessness of outer
space as clumps and streams of see-through dark matter —
the Lord G-d Y-H-W-H's redactions.

Spin

The President boasts that his very own fidget spinner,
the one for ages 12 and up, is the greatest
"Every Day Carry" ever created, ever,
the greatest, it will take his own fidget game —

diddler with paperclip and pen, no more,
in the situation room — to a new dimension.
Carbon fiber composite vortex spin,
made in the USA, of course, and adorned

with images from The Great Seal, glorious
eagle, the all-seeing eye in a triangle.
Meanwhile back in the universe, oblivious
planets, Earth, solar system, and galaxy's spiral

arms, the whole expanding shebang, illimitable
toy, billions of years distracted's a gig in a whirl.

The Wheel of Good Fortune

Someday everything will all make perfect sense.

— tweet, @fortunecookie

Believeme avows, Hidden away on the big
rock candy mountain beside a lemonade stream
is a pie that will pillow your dream. Your high-minded
principles spell success, opines **Sotrue!**
Though **Hasdonelittle** flubbed, Stop wishing and
start doing, **@real** asserts, You'll be great if you
believe in yourself, adding there is no greater
pleasure than seeing yourself and your loved ones prosper.
Bigly predicts, A short stranger will soon
enter your life with blessings to share and a fortune
in bitcoins will pile up in e-mail. **SoSad!** tsk-tsks
at the libels of **FakeNews. Everyoneknowsit** knows
everyone agrees, You are the greatest.
Nevermind **Badorsickguy** who'll whimper, The world
is your oyster, but you'll be denied its pearl.
You must sift the haystack to pinpoint the traitorous needle,
claims **Mustfindleakernow**, risking a sharp
discovery, though heroes pooh-pooh a wound, per
Sotrue!, anew. And **Buildthewall** will console,
You'll always be ringfenced by a phalanx of friends.
Then **Mustfindleakernow** chimes in again,
reminds, Failure is only the opportunity
to begin once more but more intelligently,
and **Enjoy!** rejoices, You have a flair for adding
a fanciful dimension to any story.
Covfefe concludes, sotto voce, Look,
you're a lover of words, one day you will write a book.

"It began to manifest"

It began to manifest
on otherwise unused highway billboards, huge,
the palm facing outwards, digits

alert, but what did it warn of or advertise?
Hypotheses burgeoned like roadside kudzu,
guesswork wildly coiling and climbing:

Palm reader ahead, take the next exit ramp?
Exhibit of handprints in local cave art? No outlet?
New cocoa butter hand lotion? Slow for speed hump?

One minor pundit, a maverick with a penchant
for combining stilted and colloquial diction,
opined that it was the Hand of Fate, breaking

out of its oubliette in neglected tomes
to loom over our highways, lauding
us with a high five or commanding a standstill.

Many in the bleachers felt
a quickening
when just as the final "...home of the brave" was fading,

it appeared on the stadium's Jumbotron,
its lifeline bold as the streak of a solid hit
or the arc of a rocket zooming toward Jupiter,

and offering an exceptional peek
into a future abounding with four-base wallops,
triples, and doubles, a cornucopia

for everyman's scorecard.
There wasn't even a single tweet —
surveillance data will bear this out —

concerning an alien invasion, until
as a guest on a late-night TV talk show
(already a regular on the celebrity circuit),

it cut short its riff on astrology
and began to signal
in a sign language that baffled the deaf.

But after the abduction chatter subsided,
joy went viral.
This "it" could be a media-savvy messiah,

our *manus ex machina*.

Operating on the Body Politic

The micro-surgeon sits in the waiting room
while his hands, now huge and free of him, prepare
to operate on the body politic.
Diagnosis: cancer already metastasizing
to stage 5. There's little time to spare.

After a surgeon's assistant makes the incision,
the hands begin by pre-empting visitors,
inserting bouquets of roses into the body
cavity ... no time ... the obsequies
must be intoned before the resurrection.

In a procedure guided by teleprompter,
agile fingers use avant-garde techniques
to palpate ... it's so urgent ... the limbic system,
which encircles the brainstem in a wishbone shape.
Rumors of cancer were greatly exaggerated.

But psychosurgery has penetrated
to aggression's holy grail, the amygdala,
where electrical stimulation can induce —
and here the nurses fail to check or balance —
ferocious howls from the old mammalian brain.

The hands to the micro-surgeon, "No time to spare!
Success! We've given a new voice to the older,
too-often-overlooked sub-cortical regions.
Now to excise the elites of the neo-cortex!"
Hands that strewed roses pat the orange hair.

Rumpelstilskin Rebrand

Do the old versions fit our time to a T,
as some avow? Should the Brothers Grimm have never
preserved these tellings whose whiffs of anachronism

leave us bereft of the promised gold of closure,
with only the dry stalky residue
of stock figures? — the girl, a blonde whose hair

the spotlight spun into a shimmer of wealth,
her boastful father who pimped her as sheer gold
to the bankrupt king who grew ever greedier,

and most — and least — of all, the implike creature,
the devilkin who wove himself into legend
and, itchy for the avaricious deal

but stingy with guesses, hearing his name profaned,
in his fury drove his right foot into the ground
creating a chasm into which he — and who

else? — fell, or with his bare hands tore himself —
and what besides? — in two, or in still another
unheimlich oral spin-off, flew out of the open

kitchen window on a short-handled ladle —
leaving us queasy, standing by the fairytale's
oven, sweating out the denouement.

"The midnight snacker in harlequin pj's"

The midnight snacker in harlequin pj's
tiptoes up to the cool-headed kitchen sentinel
that has stood at this post since delivery tilted it
to the station from which it will never be going AWOL.

"The door, a sentry's chest," intones this jester-
impresario, "is presto! a hero's shield
adorned with photos of everyone's happy family
and magnetized medals on which are inscribed, *Warning!*

*Failure to follow orders may result
in death, electric shock, or grievous injury!*"
Shazam! the shield morphs to the legendary
trojan horse, a nation in that appliance;

he eases open the steed and, sure enough,
as though summoned by a god, a sun clicks on
and he like a sun-god sees minuscule men
scything in fields where bread is still a gleam

in heads of wheat. This is the amber homeland,
the perdurable yet perishable dream
he feeds on, and one of his slickest tricks. Before
resealing a continent in the loam of darkness,

he checks that the control dial is set
to the transcendental chill of indefinite myth.

Deepfake ...

... AI-assisted face swapping app which takes someone's
face and places it on someone else's body

— Urban Dictionary

Our President's head sat naturally — on George
Washington's body, clad not in a regal robe
but a suit with eagle-adorned buttons — orating
on the bonus years owed to his term, with hand extended.

That head again, but orange, bewigged — on Ben
Franklin's figure, attired in jacket, vest,
and cravat, his right hand flying a kite — instructing
the nation on the lightning-strike of his victory.

Ditto but wigless with glowing, comb-over hair,
a capstone sans top hat — on Lincoln, in frock coat, trousers,
bow tie, while his big hands hang by his side — exhorting
the threatened homeland re the invading brown tide.

Encore the head, spray-tanned with white-ringed eyes —
on FDR, peerless, sporting a vintage
cape with braid fastener, velvet collar — warning
there's nothing but carnage and everything to fear.

Twin Statues

1. Statue of the Leader as Perseus

Atop his heroic nudity, a soft
cap, though rendered in marble, with rounded crown
and a stiff brim projecting from below
the logo MAGA now marmoreal.
Transfixed by that severed female head, suspended
in his left hand (his right armed with a smartphone),
he of course has turned to stone (the sculptor
was witty).
        While amid her predatory
maelstrom of hair these slithering letters — *So sad
to see! Dishonest media! O Nike!* —
seem (the illusion is uncanny) to knot
and re-knot themselves in motion. And on the plinth
this inscription, frozen:
                The hero, triumphant,
masters the fatal gaze of the feminine.

2. Statue of the Leader as St. Sebastian

His toes curl agonizingly around
the litter of smartphones at his feet, symbolic
of his historic role as notable tweeter.
The Master of Furies portrayed him as classic victim
of the libelous media's malicious elite
martyred by the barbs of outrageous chatter,

but carved an upward torque from suffering toes
to the restoration of greatness at the top
(depicting one moment of a human gesture),
as a putto, hovering over his tied hands
that are fluttering free of anonymous betrayal,
offers the wreath of heavenly redemption
in the afterlife and on earth a booming economy —
all rendered in the priceless white of ivory.

Wordslide

A tweetstorm can often trigger a deadly wordslide,
in which smithereens of speech and cliché debris
are dislodged in news outlets and social media,
some wordslides miry, like a lumbering bog,
viscous and slow, but most are avalanche-rapid,
a race to the bottom where the gloves are off
and torn to tatters in broad daylight, support
collapsing under the sheer weight of distraction,
wrecking any attempt to have a reflective
great day or nation, the dossier dirtied, the wall
advancing and we are snatched up in this fast forward
dragging us back to basics, the mass of superlative
muck that is crushing or smothering foundations
of trust, as a shifty scree of conspiracy borne
on unstable shoulders of clay is hurrying toward
a crossroad on the way to bury a country.

The Wall (running the changes)

... begins as a whisper in the orator's ear,
a wisp of concretion, a mere mnemonic standing
for all who are toxic and alien, all who are banding
together to break in and make us chant, "Build the Wall!"

The Wall is invisible but substantial, with "bricks"
made of water vapor, dust, feathers, and soot,
whatever macro and micro particles float
in the air. The Wall is both there and not there.

Each day's devoted to the walling out
of those who incessantly want to come in; however,
there's no getting around our intention to bar
their entrance. The Wall is our collective will.

Walls differ in their national character.
The Manifest Destiny of the American Wall
is horizontal but also vertical.
From the molten core, it rises to reach a star.

The Platonic Ideal of Wall can never be equaled
in *this* world. But let it inspire us to imagine
running our fingers over its unending
heavenly high-early-strength solidity.

The Wall is a political-quantum particle
that is simultaneously pure metaphor
and palpable concrete. The ingenious leader
presents this as an essential uncertainty.

It's debatable whether the rubble around the Wall
represents the remains of anti-Wall anarchy
or of those who failed to make it through, or debris
that embodies and forebodes the Wall's future.

Call it what you will — potpourri, concoction
of concrete, slatted steel, concertina wire —
The Wall is the quintessential barrier
for keeping the future out and the past in.

Walleyed. See also ...

I dreamt again of walleyed Rossie and Dickie,
twin hospital dieticians clad in white aprons
their baker's caps tilted at rakish angles,
dead now, maybe, but vivid in '63,
the year I knew them, and once again in the dream,
concocting their menus at opposite ends of Phoenix.

But face to face, a mirrorless reflection
or a macro version of the subatomic
flare-up of particle and anti-particle,
primed to vanish in an explosion of chortling,
everyone we know has rhyming names
like Sammy Kiamy [snort] and Hettel and Gettel.

In a suspended instant before detonation,
between guffaws they exhorted me to google
TheOptics.com. *Go there and click and click*
again, they confided, *because it's all connected ...*

Walleyed (colloq.) See also Exotropia
[click] —
        A condition, often metaphoric,
whose unwitting, untreated sufferers may be
immured in 2D. Their disability
is the lack of depth perception due to their eyeballs'
misalignment, so others' faces seem like walls.
A few, though untreated, may lead successful lives,
rising to an executive's office-eyrie,
relying on cues like gaudy red-and-white
and-blue's to simulate a world in 3D.
See also <u>Esotropia and Dystopia</u>

[click] ... I startled awake at an explosion
of cackling, the twins in blinding white, saying *See*
also, we told you it's all connected. See also ...

Then the Lord Answered Job Out of the Tweetstorm

So what, I did it! Afflicted you in every possible way. Just to win a bet.
Now you'll understand that the sanctimonious odor of your days, your
slaughter of time in pious ritual, is nothing to me. What the void at my
center craves — and you must agree, it's a magnificent abyss — is
absolute loyalty. No room on twitter (Sad!) for the corner-

stone of creation, much less the sea with its proud waves. Can barely
squeeze in the wilderness and the appetite of young lions. One unicorn.
A single ostrich egg. Or leave room for the glory of the horse's nostrils.
Still, my tweetstorm shows your pain's Lilliputian and cannot contend
with mine. Better get tough and smart before

it is too late! We will always have a great relationship with foreign
powers like Satan! Domestically, you and I have entered into a private
contract. Nondisclosure and no complaint. Toss the golden coin of
your loyalty into the gnawing void of creation. Any loss of goods and
family will be compensated for, abundantly.

The Speech of My Life

I delivered it from the balcony of my chin,
which I've been told is decisive and forward looking,
addressing the microbes and mites within, the countless
tribes from Staphylococcus to Demodex
that populate skin, eye, nose, throat, and intestine,
to name a few of the internal venues.

Looking toward the horizon, I waved my arms
boldly and in concert with the cogent
points I was making about unity, destiny,
and began my peroration, "You weren't mistaken
to join my campaign, selecting me to be
your singular brain and hand, your noble profile."

"I'll tell you the story of your special selves,"
I'd confided in my narration, "you who've evolved
beyond your former free-living communities
and in tandem with my warm, intuitive gut ...
we've come so far together for so long
and the State of Our Symbiotic Union is strong."

I pictured an overflow crowd that would occupy
the better part of a bucket, if smushed together,
for they are small but biblically numerous,
and as I expressed in my exordium,
appealing to ethos, per Aristotle, "I
in the greater world serve *you*: e pluribus unum."

IV.
What is Torture?

Twa Pixels

As I was walking all alane/I heard twa corbies makin a mane ...

— from the medieval ballad "Twa Corbies," in Scots dialect

As I was gazing at the TV screen,
I heard two glinting pixels gossip and scheme
in whispers, apart from the venomous debate
exploiting fear and anger at our fate.

"I'm proud to play a minor part in the spectacle,"
confided one pixel to a brother pixel.
"Though only a dot, I thrive on populist fervor;
there's no doubt rancor brightens," replied his neighbor.

"Humans invented us, and must be our God,"
said the first, "but their omni-impotence is odd.
Some kill and some incite to mayhem and riot
but many are happy to watch this, passive and quiet.

"Trapped like polar bears on tiny ice-floes
they view the calamatainment from their sofas."
"Now they believe in *us*, our shifting swarm
whose rapid, hypnotic depictions thrill and alarm."

"Who'd credit that the sinews of a gaze
could be picked so clean by flecks that dazzle and daze?"
"I almost feel pity as we teach them further
to call a crowd of pixels, like crows, a murder."

"The Husband, Children, Dog, and Lovely Wife
lean back; they're lifelike statues deprived of life,
sweetly gathered in apartment spaces
so points of light can gobble up their faces."

"In the Museum ..."

In the Museum of *On the One Hand*
But On the Other — crowned by the gilded sculpture
of Justice (blind, with sword and scales, a clone
from the courthouse) and designed for transparency
like a latter-day Victorian Crystal Palace
in plexi — torture is dealt with candidly
on an introductory panel, "What is torture? ..."
and visitors may handle a water-boarding
kit for themselves or climb inside a replica
of a "stress box" too narrow to sit down in,
too low to stand up in. A second panel
notes that a president signed off on
an "unprecedented enhanced interrogation
program" and visible in a vitrine below
are the literal embodiments of the meta-
phorical gloves the interrogators are said
to have taken off. While in a nearby alcove,
a panel asks provocatively, "Does 'enhanced
interrogation' work?" To which another
panel replies, "It depends on whom you ask.
Many think so. Others differ ..." The audio
guide pauses a moment to let you consider the pros
and cons before you proceed to the corridor
where displays, including the refrigerated snowball
once shown to the Senate and a tweet from our leader
promoting cold spells, relate to global warming.

Cairn

The hands that zealously gathered these stones are gone,
Leaving only this handless figure of stone
To point out a trail or mark a burial.

Weeping Angel,
exploit of the CIA's EDB
designed to infest smart TVs,
which in a "Fake-Off" mode are really
"on" as covert microphones.
The agency's MDB and AIB that were busy
producing malware to exfiltrate data from iPhones
and controlling malware like Assassin and Medusa.
Hammer Drill and other weaponized zero days, air
jumping viruses to infect software distributed on CDs/DVDs.
Comodo 6.x's Gaping Hole of Doom.
Cutthroat and Swindle, tools in the agency's multi-platform
Hive malware suite that attack the OS of Solaris, Windows, et al.
For cryptically pouching data on a disk — Brutal Kangaroo.
And HarpyEagle, which devoured the file systems of Apple
Airport Extreme and Airport Time capsule routers.
Fine Dining, a menu of 24 decoy applications, like a fake
virus scanner, which can be run to infect a computer or collect data.
Overall, the CIA's arsenal of numerous local and remote
zero days developed in house, obtained from the alphabet soup
of agencies, or bought from cyber arms contractors like Baitshop.

Breakthrough in a Brainstorming Session

... or what if with the back of an open hand,
fingers together, the abdomen were slapped
hard, to startle?
                                More than acceptable,
include it in the memo!
                                Clasping the head
so it's absolutely still, with a hand on either
side, fingers of course kept out of the eyes?
                                                To fix
attention! I'm sure that could be authorized.

I'm just blue-skying it, but what about
keeping the subject awake for a week while standing
stockstill in the same position?
                                That falls well
short of unbearable pain. It qualifies!

To piggyback on a previous suggestion,
why not secure the body to a board,
then cover the face with a cloth and steadily pour
water on it?
                                Perfect, what seems bizarre
will actually spark a workable solution ...

"Loudspeaker's piercing treble"

Loudspeaker's piercing treble,
staticky, urgent: "In case
the world is ending -*atick*
while you are riding the Q line
and CRACKILL! stalled in the tunnel
DO NOT CLIMB DOWN ON THE TRACK
unguided *garbled* important
DANGER from the electrified
third rail will HSSS! persist
FZZZ! after all else is destroyed
avoid SQWAUK! and follow
the conductor *mumble*." Then,
"... for your cooperation."

Loudspeaker's piercing ...

                     — God bless
this nation and what will survive us,
our values, faith, and this tapeloop —

... treble: CRACKILL! "In case ..."

These days, War ...

These days, War's a conflicted celebrity
traveling incognito, with dark glasses
over which he coyly peeks to see
if anyone notices him as he gorges himself
on ribs in the booth of an upscale eatery
or waits on line at the airport, casting himself
as a mega-hero again, daydreaming a movie
in which *I alone survive the massive destruction*
of every friend or anonymous enemy.

Nowadays, War masquerades as a junior Einstein,
a tousled, techy, down-to-earth intellect
who has deduced the death of the straight line
and the obsolescence of space as a single stage
tick-tocked by a universal time.
Instead, we're blessed with a myriad now's and spaces
in which the dying and wounded howl and writhe
each a reference-body for calculating
the equations of physics for a stricken I.

Currently, War portrays himself as victim
not conqueror: *Think of me as one*
of the countless homeless, he whines, *like her or him,*
ubiquitous and invisible, though sprawled
in plain view, regrettable spew of a system
whose battlefield is near, as well as far
and extolled by your patriotic anthem or hymn,
which is only the blanket that covers a casualty. Yes,
ignore me as you hum on the way to your gym.

These days, War is *fed up with bad press*
that emphasizes my destructive side,
and you can quote me on this. I want to stress
all the good I promote: negotiation
among nations, for instance, and proper dress
and elegant manners, mostly, at conferences.
So what if it takes a few mortar rounds, more or less,
to fire up the desire for peace. Motivation's
the key, and my argument's cogent. I trust I impress.

Words for a Cenotaph for Words

Stranger, you are facing the vacant grave
Honoring acronyms and words so brave
They sacrificed their last measure of meaning
In the War on Terror, but let there be kudos, not keening,
For letters that answered the call of our nation's fears
And battled in secret for myriads of years:

EKIA, who created a category,
The wide-open, welcoming "enemy killed in action,"
Your linking of nameless bodies to a faction
Was vital to our collateral damage story
And earned you eternal bureaucratic glory.

Find, Fix, and Finish, a kinetic trio
Your tenacity was legend in e-mail and memo,
Whether exhibited in application
To targeted kills or to family and avocation.

Indefinite Detainee, with legal prowess
You circumvented a tedious justice process
By arguing for a legalistic limbo
To correspond with a brick-and-mortar Gitmo.
Detained in figurative dust, may you Rest in Peace.

Jackpot, the jokester, you will be sorely missed
Who in your christening of successful kills
Combined the gifts of gambler and ironist.
Your humor made bearable war's unavoidable ills.

Kill Chain, who knew how to pass a fatal decision
To a superior with speed and precision,
Until the no or yes was up to POTUS,
Your deeds will be passed down, with veneration,
To every brave new succeeding generation.

Belovèd *Reaper,* not grim and nearly blithe
With the buoyant spirit of an unmanned scythe,
You helped us garner joyful victory
Virtually unscathed by casualty.

Stranger, in our secure and peaceful time,
These warrior words have entered the sublime
Of the homeland's everlasting verbal hoard
On the internet's vast cyber bulletin board.
Their cenotaph's silent, to hear them spoken aloud,
You can download the Valhalla App from iCloud.

The New Arcimboldo

cued in by the docent we do a double take
at the coiffure
those man-curls are circular razor wire

and the eyes, we're informed, are combat goggles
permitting the subject to process
both normal and infrared optics
so he'll never be blindsided in the field
by overlooked objects

ears, a pair of parabolic antennae
directing/receiving radio waves
in pulses from ships, planes, and guided missiles
but capable too of echo-locating
the scribbled signature of a hurled grenade

cheeks are the latest armor, highly tensile
metal face plates, relatively thin,
made of depleted uranium
with a stubble beard of barbs from the wire
that prickled No Man's Land in the Great War

we're led to notice the forward-deployed tactical nose
a nuclear bomb with a 50-kiloton sneeze

and are told the mouth is the pursed "o"
of a submachine gun's muzzle
to patter out high-caliber ideas

the belligerent chin
juts with the confidence
of a substance harder than diamond
light-gray polycrystalline wurtzite bn
a superabrasive spewed in volcanic eruption

and then it's suggested we note the neck
a circular wall of concrete, ultra thick
guarding the nation of the head and face
at the border with the upper torso

Boutique Warfare

The House of Creech will debut a stunning new line
of MQ-9 Reapers, designed for the minimal
collateral wear-and-tear of boutique warfare
and accessorized with a host of goodies on fleek,
like the Hellfire II air-to-ground missile
and the Paveway II laser-guided payload.

Nor will this fabled House neglect the local,
downscale consumer, offering an array
of fashion knock-offs, like the asymmetric
top with dislocated fastener, Semtex
sweater, and "Vitriol" and "Obsession" dresses.

Top-secret plans for window-displays, it is whispered,
will feature the concept, High-Tech Fashion Invasion,
with a group of gaunt manikins seemingly menaced
by a swooping wave of vermilion paper planes.

High-End Germanic Forest

Bold concept in home design — the living room re-
conceived for our time as a pristine, primeval clearing
in a faux but frisson-inducing Germanic forest.

This high-end design, composed of dappled light,
earth color, and wild boar wallpaper, all colliding
at different levels to frame a fantasy zone,
is a breakthrough in line with what gurus assert is the new
demolition of the indoor-outdoor barrier.

With an open-hearth kitchen, cooking, eating, and lounging
blend in an energetic flow as if geared
for the imminent arrival of wolf or woodman,
while surrounding the clearing stand the ancient/modern
ICBMs-cum-neoclassical columns
whose metal skin is skillfully camouflaged
as beech or oak and whose warheads are cached within
an aluminum honeycomb sheathed in a pyrolitic
carbon-epoxy composite for re-entry.

Dancing flames in the double-sided fireplace
prove coziness and spaciousness co-exist,
and bibelots like aluminized balloons
that serve to confuse interception radars
bring authenticity to the owners' journey
of self-discovery. Relish the al fresco
aura with family, certain your fantasy's earned.

The Kill Shelter

"The pleasant land of counterpane."

— Robert Louis Stevenson

Dwell in softness, like sleeping on a cloud
that dreamlike drifts above the fertile earth
in our Deco Faux Leather Daybed and Trundle,
with goose down pillows and superlight designer
rifle. You are protected by a perpetual
guarantee for the mattress's ten layers
and the more than ten pounds' worth of cashmere, mohair,
silk, and alpaca. Moreover, the rifle's barrel
aligns with the stock, reducing the stress of recoil.
Lost in a reverie and buoyed up by thousands
of pocketed coils, made of Vanadium steel,
adjustable to your chosen tension, recall
in comfort how this handmade cloud was crafted
on Plymouth's rocky coast and trust in the gun's
smooth operation in automatic mode.
Perks include a back-up mattress of foam
that remembers your body and a Picatinny
rail for the rifle with add-ons like laser sight,
bipod, flashlight, bible, and bayonet.

Sunday in the Park

How sweet to stroll through the Garden of Gestures at sunrise
in Humanity Memorial Park. As you enter
the Alley of Shrugging Shoulders lined on left
and right by videos of headless torsos
miming "unsolvable problem, what can one do?"
the sun will bathe your face in radiant light.

Pause at the rolling Meadows of Futility
where a scatter of scarecrows with wisps of straw representing
their open palms extended to the side
are attired in Prada, Chanel, and de la Renta —
hung-over guardians of bonhomie,
feeling under the weather, far and wide.

Bring your own lunch and at noontime eat by the Fountain
of Flood and Drought where a plaque admonishes,
"Beware, the water!" Admire the verdigrised sculptures
of water-seekers that warily circle the basin,
lion, lamb, and little child, frozen
together in need, refugees from the Peaceable Kingdom.

Toward evening the vacant bandshell stage will feature
a lightshow from the situation room's
computer screens and tv's with politicians
pantomiming orations as the strains
of martial music can almost be heard in the darkening
silence concluding your Sunday in the park.

V.
Rules of the Game

Sending a Clear and Unmistakable Message

The U.S. is sending a carrier group to the Middle East ahead
of schedule ... — AP, 5/6/19

Proper deportment heightens security
(despite the d-word's charm-school connotation),
especially in regard to the provocation
of unspecified but troubling and escalatory

indications and warnings that on land
and sea, proxies are rising up and re-
positioning. Answer with poise and a policy
of exerting purposeful and prudent command

and demonstrating a light but determined footfall
with unrelenting force. Even a modest
adjustment in deploying significant assets
(for example, gliding like a gazelle, but fully

alert, to a forward position) can effect
an optimum realignment. Projecting power
by means of your confident bearing (no glowering
needed, just easy breathing) will correct

any defects in deportment and lead to your standing
taller in a heightened security posture.

The Loss of Little Boy

Psychologists say the early loss of a sibling
can have profound inimical effects.
Take the case of Little Boy, America's

baby brother, who lived for only days.
I can almost picture him growing up, a towhead
flicking bottle-caps in a game of skully

or knuckling the pocket of his baseball mitt ...
but he perished in a violent metastasis —
be brave just once to recall the bitter details,

they say — in a flash that seared the flesh to shadow.
At first, on Tinian Island, he was tended
and protected by teams of youthful American men,

vigilant, though the heat was certainly severe
and the set-up more like a spartan all-male resort
than a hospital. What kind of nurses were these

who lifted him into the care of a Superfortress
named for the pilot's mother, only to be
released six miles above an unaware city,

plummeting faster than fear to his death in mid-air?
Psychologists say, to combat survivor guilt
focus on pleasant connections with the lost one,

on recollections with viable life lessons.

Nuclear Croquet

A critical technique of this game is movement
in the line of aim, so the strike is executed
smoothly, without hesitation, moving all body
parts in the desired direction. Depending
on how much power is required, the main
"firing" command is relayed from thigh muscles
through back and arm and via the wrist to the hand.

Surprisingly, a somnambulist best embodies
the almost mystic ideal of total engagement
known as the Flow state, achieving greater
accuracy and control than a waking player.

Research confirms that sleepers can perform
a sequence of complex behaviors and tasks, including,
despite an apparently glazed, unseeing expression,
the trick of retaining a final, decisive look
at the target and bringing this picture back to the striking
zone to ensure that the "missile" is well and truly
addressed. That image doesn't last long and so
the strike must be initiated quickly.

We can regard the world as the nation's backyard
for the purposes of the game, with string or chalk
together with flags defining the field of play
(all flesh is grass for this lawn) and a deadness board
to record a striker's progress. Irregular patches
like the Caucasus mountains are not an obstacle,
wickets can double as archways to populous cities,
and stockpiles of mallets and balls are plentiful.

Nuclear Etiquette

The rules of nuclear etiquette are based
on pragmatism, good manners, and common sense:
Never refer to the first fission device
by nickname as "Gadget," unless you are old friends.

Protocol is not an end in itself,
but fosters exchanges that are diplomatic:
Do not introduce a fusion device as "Mark"
sans "Thermonuclear," the honorific.

Further: in going through doorways, the Swann-implosion-
device and its party of highly-valued kin,
e.g. Robin, Tsetse, Python, and Kimono,
are always the first out and the first in.

Selecting a gift for the Genie air-to-air-rocket
is tricky. Even the type, color, and number
of items may hint at an unintended meaning.
Mums, for instance, can be a funeral flower.

When offering a toast to the Violet Mist
nuclear land mine, rise in place and address
the entire room. Then raising your glass, be sure
to look directly at the honored guest.

Leavetakings, greetings, telephone conversations,
seating arrangement, suitable gift or pet,
cutlery — there's little that won't fall
within the domain of nuclear etiquette.

Nuclear Volleyball

A foundational sport for opposing countries that show
teamwork on a global court with an ocean
preempting the typical polyester net.
Hitter, middle blocker, setter poised
in a tableau vivant of readiness.
                                        However,
per intricate protocols, and in all fairness
the game will only begin when a stealth bomber
whose radar signature is no bigger
than a volleyball is sent aloft, or served,
initiating a rally, and instantly
competitors will abandon frozen positions
and rapidly put into play — with the utmost respect
for the opposition and abiding by protocols —
a multitude of "volleyballs," with a launch
initially lifting each ball into the air,
followed by the set, or aim, and the spike,
a savage overhead attacking shot.

Power is a vital component in ending
a rally, and coaches continue to devise
new strategies, tactics, and skills in this game of constant
motion whose first match has yet to be played.

Forecast

Even in the widespread valley fog
caused by auspicious radiating conditions
and wet soil, the President will not lose
sight of his "shadow," the officer-silhouette
toting the pigskin whose innards are top secret.

Though water vapor imagery depicts
only a gradual approach of an upstream
short wave and heavy overcast will be slow
to depart, the nuclear bomb's core and trigger,
stored separately, can be fetched for assembly pronto.

Despite a low amplitude ridge of high pressure
that will give way to a more zonal pattern
with a diffuse system and an unsteady
dry front, the long-range bombers with pre-armed
nuclear bombs are always aloft and ready.

Although the southern edge of the westerlies
will get close enough to introduce high thin clouds
but the low to mid levels will remain
too dry to support any precipitation,
the codes could still be transmitted, for inundation.

Le Dernier Cri

It is 1945 and Fat Man strides
down the fashion runway, confidently
sporting the latest in Army Air Force attire,
a cotton khaki shade number 1 uniform
custom-tailored to fit his fabled torso.

Eyes on an imaginary horizon,
he hardly deigns to notice the oohs and ahs,
the awestruck admiration of those below.

Nearly to the end, he pauses, allows
the audience to sense the full impact
of his odd but avant-garde figure and even observe
the Air Corps emblem on his shoulder, a blue
circle containing a winged white five-pointed star,
centered in which is a red disk, "the meatball."

As if halted in freefall, he hovers above onlookers
while flashbulbs of the paparazzi pop.

Then pivots, returns, as if he hasn't heard
or seen a thing. Face, an implacable mask.
Returns behind the curtain, where, unseen
by the crowd, and extending back far into our future,
a line of supermodels wait for their turn
to make a debut, launching new eras in fashion.
Beginning with Mark 4 and the dream of clean
subdued lines of a pure blue uniform ...

Singularities in Everyday Life

In boyhood's galactic epoch, outer space
began at my feet, and singularities
were a frequent phenomenon. They freckled
the TV screen as pixels, gobbling attention
most when they clustered to form personalities
like Pinky Lee, Lucy, and Buffalo Bob,
leaving as residue on the event horizon
our couch-bound bodies. Also, the speckled blue
linoleum on my bedroom floor, a flattened
infinity, was riddled with many micro-
black holes that swallowed up hosts of plastic soldiers
as my bare knees rested atop a billion stars.

But the optimum region for the generation
of collapsed supergravitational matter
was mom and dad's closet, where singularities
like moths were fashioning gaps in dresses and suits.
From the absence of bodies and the array of personae
dangling from hangers, I detected a cosmic
crime scene, confirmed by the serried ranks of empty
shoes whispering, conspiring to step out
on their own in the universe. Black holes were pul-
lulating throughout my life and one even crushed
my formidable grandpa gripped by its minute
supermassive deformed region of spacetime.

Diary of a Transformed Deity

for my sister, Lillian Israel

Monday, I wakened from my voluminous snooze
startled to find I'd morphed into a Market,
my sacred pneuma now dispersed in flows
of cash and commodities. I was in bits,
but ubiquitous, passed from hand to hand like the shards
of a relic, and subject to a novel symptom,
volatility.
   Tuesday, the exuberant
adoration of the traders was reassuring,
but what of the programmed "hymns" of the algorithms?

I was getting good press on Wednesday, except
for a few heretics, pseudo market gurus
claiming the faith bubble had popped, spooking
the skittish investors, inciting the pursuit
of false profits in panic-driven selloffs.

Thursday, consulted my (financial) analyst,
re the obsessive notion that I never
had woken, but only fallen into a deeper
dream, so these tremors and fluctuations occurred
as electrical impulses in my cosmic neurons
while my exterior was calmly iconic.

Friday, I have fond memories of my future,
perfumed with the incense of adrenalin,
my myth preserved in the gospel of the tremulous,
I've become an affliction that's far too big to fail.

Old Man Icarus

Impetuous boy trapped in an old man's body,
he recalls in a flash the alluring dazzle of height,
the pungent burning wax, the tightly meshed
feathers scattering, and the stomach-churning
headfirst fall — as he carefully navigates
a step's descent from the high curb to the street.
Later, he sits on a bench in the park and flicks
a crumb at his favorite ground-hugging urban bird

and feels himself a crumb left over from myth,
humble and real, like a meager pellet of bread.
Surprising survivor — a passing boat, too minor
to be in the story, rescued the boy who tumbled
out of legend into the random world,
leaving the indelible streak of his fall
as an instant signature and perpetual lesson.

In dreams that dizzy fall dissolves to the spin
of a record on which his father performs an aria
of incitements and cautions: Be passionate, but fear
the sun, great heights, memory — all the spavining
phobias caught up in the song, melodic
lesson incised by the smell of melting wax.

On a cedar-perfumed porch, he inhabits a rocking-
chair, the one with a scorched wing attached
on either side — yes, he saved these when
the good fishermen hauled him, half-dead, out of
the sea. Blackened, dear, bitter mementos.

Rocking, he feels he is migrating in his chair
over a vast sea, father in the lead
again, ingenious dot on the horizon,
busy inventing more and more vacancy.

The Battle of the Bulge

Conceived as the world was ripped by cataclysm,
I was at first a solipsist, immersed
in the amniotic puddle, alerted or lulled
by a heartbeat that was jittery or stable,
submerged in her and believing we were I.

A dog's barking and a lawnmower's drone,
the music of sporadic conversation,
and the muffled roar of the crowds at a stadium
were part of me and all I knew of war,
sounds without sources, heard through her rushing blood.

A conscripted soul, I was being equipped
with a regulation brain, a spinal cord,
and millions of synapses for the liberation.
I overheard a radio's Marseillaise
reverberating through the bones of her body.

Later, I caught the authoritative tones
of bulletins on The Battle of the Bulge,
and though ignorant of military strategy,
I mastered the tactics of flutter and kick. But afloat
in her, I couldn't, like a soldier, crawl on my belly.

While GI's froze in the forest called Ardennes,
half-starved, having outrun their line of supply
(I was tethered to mine), crouching in foxholes
or crossing snowy fields into fields of fire,
I was snug in her underwater dark.

A fetus, I was innocent of the risks
of a siege enforced by a German panzer corps,
and the peril of being deployed in a mother's body
or of being born. On December 23rd,
the weather cleared, though in her it was still murky,

and allied planes retook the skies. I drifted
on unknowing what was above or below.
Then Patton's armor broke their lines and I
would soon assault the breach, in a difficult birth —
new blood and guts — to bawl at her in the light.

Notes

The acrostic poem "What Goes Around ..." parodies, and uses language from, Lewis Carroll's "A Boat Beneath a Sunny Sky."

"Voice" borrows language from the article "Working vocal cords grown from human cells," by Ian Sample (*The Guardian*, November 18, 2015).

"In the Museum ..." uses and adapts language from the article "Now kids, help us to kill Bin Laden! The dark side of Washington's spy museum," by David Smith (*The Guardian*, May 27, 2019).

"Cairn" borrows language from the article "With WikiLeaks Claims of C.I.A. Hacking, How Vulnerable Is Your Smartphone?," by Steve Lohr and Katie Benner (*New York Times*, March 7, 2017).

"The Battle of the Bulge": "Old blood and guts" was a nickname for General Patton.

Acknowledgments

Thanks are due to the editors of the following journals and anthologies, where these poems will appear or have appeared, sometimes in earlier versions:

JOURNALS

5x5: "Diary of a Transformed Deity"; *American Journal of Poetry:* "The Battle of the Bulge"; *Barrow Street:* "An Ethnographic Fieldnote"; "The Wheel of Good Fortune"; *BigCityLit:* "Singularities in Everyday Life"; "Sunday in the Park"; *Dispatches from the Poetry Wars,* June 2018: "Operating on the Body Politic"; "The midnight snacker in harlequin pj's"; "Rumpelstilskin Rebrand"; "Walleyed. See also ..."; "Cairn"; *Hamilton Stone Review:* "A Favorite Indoor Sport"; "A Graveyard of Past Futures"; "A Singular Sect"; "An Issue for Further Research"; "An Age of Diplomacy"; *The High Window* #3 (UK): "Voice" (re-print); *Jewish Currents:* "The Loss of Little Boy"; *Lampeter Review* (UK): "Voice"; *The North* (UK), Issue 60: "Spin"; "A Planetary Pastime" (as "Among the Gliesians"); *Offcourse* #70: "Redaction"; "Breakthrough in a Brainstorming Session"; "Loudspeaker's Piercing Treble"; "These Days, War ..."; and "Words for a Cenotaph for Words"; *Pembroke Magazine:* "Old Man Icarus"; *Pennsylvania Literary Journal:* "Deepfake"; "In the Museum ..."; "Sending a Clear and Unmistakable Message"; *Plume:* "Nuclear Etiquette"; *Poetry Salzburg 32:* "The New Arcimboldo"; "Boutique Warfare"; *Portside.org:* "Forecast" (re-posted); "Operating on the Body Politic" (re-posted); "The Wall (running the changes)"; *Scoundrel Time:* "Then the Lord Answered Job Out of the Tweetstorm"; "Statue of the Leader as Perseus"; *Terrain.org,* Letter to America series: "Forecast"; *The Main Street Rag:* "The Speech of My Life"; *The RavensPerch:* "Nuclear Croquet"; "Nuclear Volleyball"; "Statue of the Leader as Saint Sebastian"; *Wild Court* (UK): "Twa Pixels"

ANTHOLOGIES

45 Poems of Protest, edited by Kirk Ramdath (Eleventh Transmission, Canada): "The Wall (running the changes)" (re-post)

Four American Poets, edited by Anthony Costello (The High Window Press, UK): "Voice" (re-print); "Man's Best Friend"; "What Goes Around"; "Print the Legend"; "How Often Must We Repeat ..."; "Jumping the Gun"; "Creative Policing"

Like Light: 25 Years of Poetry and Prose, edited by Bertha Rogers: "High-End Germanic Forest"; "The Kill Shelter"

Plume Anthology #5: "Fabricating Uncertainty"

Resist Much, Obey Little (Dispatches Editions, 2017): "It began to manifest"

I would like to express my gratitude to Mark Sullivan and D. Nurkse for reading an earlier version of my manuscript and generously offering their editorial advice. I am also deeply grateful to Jessie Lendennie, my publisher, for her unstinting support and to Siobhán Hutson for her creative book designs.

PHILIP FRIED has published seven previous collections of poetry, including *Squaring the Circle* (Salmon, 2017), *Interrogating Water* (Salmon, 2014), and *Early/Late: New and Selected Poems* (Salmon, 2011). In addition to writing poetry, he edits *The Manhattan Review,* an international poetry journal he founded in 1980. Fried lives in New York with his wife, the fine-art photographer Lynn Saville.